a year in the life

The Mendip Hills

Photographs by

John Bailey   *Tina Bailey*

DB
PUBLISHING

Mells, the quintessential English village, where several quiet country lanes meet from the hamlets of Great Elm, Vobster, Egford and the village of Buckland Dinham.

Contents

Priddy Mineries, located high on Western Mendip, create a deeply mysterious atmosphere.

Introduction

Somersetshire is a hilly county: in the North the great range of the Mendip Hills extends from a little south-westward of Frome to Hutton to the south of Weston-super-mare, a distance of about 25 miles.

Taken from *Kelly's Directory*, 1902

The Mendip Hills, or Mendips, were formed over 300 million years ago. Carboniferous limestone was laid down as the result of sediment from aquatic life in a warm sea and the area was then subjected to folding and uplifting, resulting in the landscape we see today. The nature of the limestone allows water to percolate down, the resulting erosion forming a vast labyrinth of caves, caverns and underground rivers, most notably at Wookey Hole and Cheddar. There are many other caves but most are unknown to any but a few of the experienced cavers who explore in the Mendip Hills. The summit of the limestone ridge affords spectacular views north-west over the Severn Estuary to Wales and west across the Somerset Levels to Exmoor. Mellow stone villages connected by quiet country lanes complement the picturesque valleys carved from the limestone by the force of water over millions of years.

Ask any visitor about the Mendips and they will talk of Cheddar Gorge and Burrington Combe and rightly so: these natural features are a spectacular sight to behold. However, Mendip has a far greater diversity of beauty and ruggedness than these two giants. This book reveals the true extent of the variety of the countryside and villages that nestle among the contours of the Mendips Hills, many with traditions that can be traced back over the centuries.

The highest point of the plateau, Beacon Batch at 1,068ft, lies south of Burrington Combe. Over 80 square miles of western Mendip has now been designated as an Area of Outstanding Natural Beauty. To the south lie Wells, Glastonbury and the Somerset Levels, and to the north the Avon Valley, linking the maritime city of Bristol and the Georgian city of Bath.

Past industrial activity has played a large part in the landscape of Mendip, and our Bronze Age, Iron Age and Roman ancestors all left their mark on the countryside. The Victorians continued the trend through lead mining, and modern-day stone quarrying for road-building is still an important part of industrial activity in the region. In 1874 the Somerset & Dorset Railway laid a track across the Mendips which reached its highest point on the line from Bath to Bournemouth at Maesbury. Sadly closed as a consequence of the Beeching axe in 1966, evidence of the line remains today.

This book portrays a year in the life of the unspoilt villages, quiet country lanes, valleys, hills and spectacular gorges of the Mendip Hills. The journey begins on the western fringes where the hills rise abruptly from the Somerset Levels, soon to reach the highest point at Beacon Batch. The limestone ridge continues eastward, where the limestone grasslands and exposed rocks steadily give way to the more gentle landscape of the winding lanes and wooded valleys of eastern Mendip. Due to the height above sea level winter can be far more harsh here than in the surrounding lowlands that are just a few miles distant. Mendip is often overlooked by residents of the many towns and villages that grew up on the spring lines at the foot of the hills, and by the numerous travellers on their journey down the busy M5 motorway to the south coast.

Part One:
Western Mendip

The parish church of St Andrew sits in a tranquil combe on the western edge of Mendip.

A fine lantern adorns the entrance to the church.

Compton Bishop

The village of Compton Bishop nestles in a combe on the extreme south-western slopes of the Mendip Hills. The starting point for our journey east across the carboniferous limestone ridge begins here in an Area of Outstanding Natural Beauty.

In the heart of the village, overlooked by Crook Peak and Wavering Down, is the parish church of St Andrew, which was consecrated in 1236, although it is believed that a church stood on the site from earlier times. Impressive church towers are a dominant feature of Mendip villages, and St Andrew's is no exception to that tradition.

The area was once home to prosperous apple orchards, but these have long gone. Nevertheless, agriculture continues with the slopes above the village providing rich grazing for cattle and sheep, as they have done for centuries. Like many of the villages we shall encounter on the journey, the settlement of Cross, part of the same parish, was once home to three coaching inns serving travellers on their passage through Somerset via the Bristol to Bridgwater turnpike road. The traditional village blacksmith and wheelwright would have been located close at hand.

The south doorway dates from Norman times.

The south doorway and the font at St Andrew's date from Norman times, made almost a century before the dedication of the church in 1236. Inside is a superb example of a 14th-century carved stone pulpit, believed to be one of the finest in Somerset. An oak chest that once belonged to the churchwarden is located in the centre of the nave and would have once contained a slot where money for the poor of the parish could have been left.

Sunlight enhances the mellow stone.

A large crop of holly berries is said to signify a hard winter ahead.

Holly trees can be seen growing in many churchyards, and a fine example can be seen at St Andrew's. Folklore suggests that they were planted to offer protection from lightning strikes and, according to modern-day science, the theory worked, as the spines on the leaves can act as miniature lightning conductors, thus giving protection to both the tree and the immediate surroundings. Tradition also has it that planting a holly bush outside a house would ward off storms, while builders incorporated the wood into houses' doorsteps to prevent witches from entering. The red berries are only found on the female tree, providing an important food supply for wild birds during winter months. Large crops of berries are said to be an indication of a hard winter ahead, but it is more likely to be the result of a good summer the previous year.

The tradition of holly being brought into the house at Christmas is associated with the darkest part of the year and the rebirth of the sun after the winter solstice on 21 December.

The summit of Crook Peak dominates the skyline above Compton Bishop.

Looking east across Mendip from the limestone outcrop of Crook Peak.

12

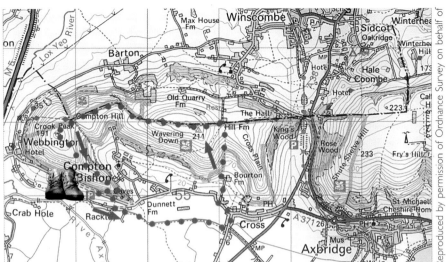

Crook Peak Walk

Distance: 5 miles with an estimated time of 2.5–3 hours.

The bulk of the Mendip Hills are made up of an undulating limestone plateau, but at Crook Peak the limestone breaks through to provide a genuine summit with an uninterrupted view in all directions.

The walk begins at the car park on the Webbington Road at grid reference 392 550, with one very steep section on the climb to Wavering Down. Some paths can become muddy after a spell of heavy rain.

The route begins by heading east along the Webbington Road for 400 yards before taking a path on your right, descending to emerge onto Rackley Lane. Turn left onto the lane then right down a track after a short distance to cross the Cheddar Yeo. At this point you are little more than 20ft above sea level. Cross a stile to follow the river, keeping the bank on your left for just over a mile. The path guides you along the northern edge of the Somerset Levels in complete contrast to the loftier part of the route to come. The path alongside the river provides for easy walking with some stiles to cross, but take time to admire the excellent views of the Mendip escarpment. Cross a stile by a delightful road bridge, taking a left turn onto the Old Coach Road that brings you into the village of Cross.

The Cheddar Yeo is your tranquil companion for the first part of the walk.

The stone wall clearly defines the path across Wavering Down.

The trig point sits 676ft above sea level on Wavering Down.

The village was once home to three coaching inns supplying refreshment and rest for weary travellers, who would have included Samuel Coleridge and Wordsworth. Why not do as they would have done and take a rest prior to moving on? Once refreshed, head west along the Webbington Road from the junction with the Old Coach Road for 250 yards before taking a right turn into Bourton Lane. In a short distance, at Bourton Farm, turn left following a track past a cottage to emerge on the hillside. The route bears right at the end of the track, and once through a gate on your left it becomes quite steep as the climb up the Mendip escarpment begins. When you reach Hill Farm turn left following a stone wall on your right to reach Wavering Down with its trig point at 676ft above sea level.

Trig points, or triangulation pillars, were built to assist an accurate geographical survey of Great Britain that began in 1935. In some low-lying areas trig points may be only a few feet above sea level. The positioning of the trig points was such that at least two others could be seen from any one. By sitting a theodolite on the concealed mountings on top of the pillars an accurate bearing to the nearest trig points could be taken. This process, called triangulation, covered the whole country and led to the production of the OS (Ordnance Survey) maps we use today.

The concealed mountings on top of triangulation pillars were used to accommodate a theodolite to obtain accurate readings.

You have now joined for a short while the long-distance footpath called the West Mendip Way, a 30-mile route across the southern edge of Mendip from Wells to the sea at Uphill. Continue following the stone wall downhill until you reach a path that bears left to the clearly visible summit of Crook Peak.

The view on a clear day may keep you here for some time, with the Bristol Channel and the Brecon Beacons clearly visible. Closer, seemingly almost within touching distance, the M5 motorway snakes its way north and south far below. To the east the bulk of Mendip stands proud above the beautiful Somerset countryside.

The final part of the route now takes a south-south-east direction down the southern side of the summit, with easy walking on short turf. Far below is the village of Compton Bishop, where the Church of St Andrew dominates the scene. The route continues for three quarters of a mile before reaching a wooden open stile and woodland. Take the path leading away to the right, heading west and eventually emerging to find the car park on the opposite side of the road.

Compton Hill and Crook Peak viewed from Wavering Down.

The view west from Crook Peak takes in Brean Down, a limestone outlier, and the island of Steep Holme, with the coast of South Wales in the far distance.

The limestone outlier of Nyland Hill rises to just over 230ft, a giant in comparison to the surrounding low-lying Somerset Levels. In the distance is the unmistakable outline of Glastonbury Tor.

Axbridge

A panorama of the southern slopes of the Mendip escarpment can be viewed from the reservoir close to Axbridge. The carboniferous limestone of the Mendips allows water to percolate through the rocks, emerging as springs at the foot of the hills. The lack of surface water was the reason that the western plateau remained sparsely populated, with the major areas of habitation growing up around the spring lines at the foot of the hills, the exception being Priddy. The sources of water have now been tapped and the area below Mendip boasts three large reservoirs. To the north lie Blagdon Lake, completed in 1901, and Chew Valley Lake, completed in 1956. To the south at Axbridge lies Cheddar Reservoir, completed in 1937 and fed by the springs that emerge at the foot of the gorge. The capacity of the reservoir is a staggering 1,350 million gallons, and it serves an area stretching from Tetbury in Gloucestershire to south of Glastonbury.

The Mendip escarpment looking out east from the Cheddar Reservoir at Axbridge. The wooded slopes below the ridge are beginning to sport their autumn colours.

The edge of the icy cold waters is patrolled by the Redshank, walking at a steady brisk pace to find food.

The reservoir attracts a variety of wildfowl and birds during the winter, although not on the scale of Chew Valley Lake. One striking visitor is the Redshank, a resident of Britain, although many more winter here with over half those numbers migrating from Iceland. The Redshank is a common wader of coasts, estuaries and marshes, but it is also at home here on the edge of the reservoir at Cheddar. They feed by patrolling rocky or muddy shorelines, walking at a fast pace and pecking at the surface, finding food by sight. They breed in June and are monogamous, with pairs returning to the same site each year.

A closer look at the upland area above Cheddar from the reservoir. This time, in the depths of winter, the Mendips are sporting their winter coat. This was a particularly cold spell with temperatures falling several degrees below freezing, with the resultant snow also falling at the lower levels. The sky above is beginning to fill with moisture, threatening to continue the winter's icy grip with another blanket of snow.

Cheddar Gorge

Cheddar Gorge was formed as a result of meltwater floods over several arctic periods during the last million years. The Mendips were periglacial, bordering a glacial area, but were not themselves covered in ice all year. The melting snow during the brief summer months was forced over the surface, eroding the vast limestone gorge we see today. The water that once percolated the limestone now continues to run below the surface, having created a labyrinth of caves and underground rivers: a sight to be marvelled at beneath the Mendips. The spectacular underground world has created a haven for cavers, with Cheddar Caves accessible to all.

The gorge itself is a spectacular sight equal to any upland area of England, only perhaps on a smaller scale. The cliff edge rises vertically to a height of 450ft above the winding B3135 as its snakes its way through the gorge. The limestone cliffs can be accessed by climbing Jacob's Ladder on the southern escarpment which gives a view of the gorge and the land to the west, taking in the Somerset Levels and the Bristol Channel. The north cliffs are accessed from the village, where a path continues upward through Black Rock and Velvet Bottom to emerge high on the Mendip plateau at Charterhouse.

The gorge was formed as a result of meltwater floods over the last million years.

Soay sheep have been introduced to graze the grassland and scrub of the steep slopes of the gorge.

The area beneath the tall cliffs where the road is forced into a series of twists and turns is a popular area for rock climbers.

Present-day Cheddar is now home to some Soay sheep introduced to graze the grassland and scrub that grows on the slopes of the gorge and the limestone cliffs. Soay sheep originate from the islands of the St Kilda archipelago, a group of islands some 41 miles west of the Outer Hebrides. They are believed to be the oldest breed of domestic sheep.

On 10 July 1968 the Mendip area was hit by extraordinarily heavy rain, and Cheddar Gorge was once again transformed into a raging torrent. The rains were said to be the worst in living memory. Several thousand tons of rock and scree were washed from the cliffs down the gorge, with major flooding caused to many shops and houses and the caves themselves. Over half a mile of the gorge road was torn up, with holes made in the ground up to 30ft deep and other parts buried under tons of rock, scree and mud.

From Saxon times Cheddar and the surrounding land was a royal hunting forest. The land was given to the Bishop of Bath and Wells in 1204 by King John. It was subsequently deforested and used as grazing land for sheep and goats. Grazing sheep on the slopes and plateau eventually became uneconomic in the 1920s and the landscape once again underwent a change, with bracken and gorse growing profusely, particularly on the plateau areas above the gorge. The limestone grasslands still support several rare wild flowers, including Cheddar Pinks.

The gorge with the early morning sun highlighting the northern cliffs. Beyond the gorge the average height of the surrounding countryside is only 20ft above sea level, in stark contrast to the Mendip Hills.

The unique limestone grasslands support a variety of rare wild flowers and plants.

A calm summer's day in the gorge, a far cry from the deluge of 1968.

Heavy snow can fall on the higher plateau, but it seldom lasts more than a few days.

A heavy fall of snow can transform the hills into a winter wonderland, but brings transport chaos to the country lanes of Mendip. Winter on Mendip can be in stark contrast to the nearby lower-lying areas that are just a few miles distant. Snow can accumulate on the Mendips while rain falls on the surrounding areas, which are lower than 300ft above sea level. The reason for this variation in weather is due to air temperature being reduced by one degree for every 330ft of elevation. Snow rarely falls if the temperature is above 2 degrees, so with an ambient temperature of 4 degrees at 300ft it is less than 2 degrees on the highest part of Mendip, with precipitation as snow rather than rain. Snow is created inside clouds as tiny ice crystals. The snowflakes melt on their way to the ground and fall as rain, except when the air temperature at ground level is cold enough.

Wind-blown snow on the exposed lanes of Mendip creates a captivating scene, but can disrupt traffic.

Probably the best time to view the rock formation of the gorge is in midwinter, when the skies have cleared after a dusting of snow.

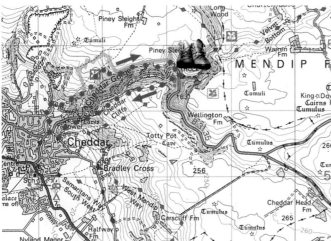

Cheddar Walk

Distance: 4 miles with an estimated time of 3 hours.

The walk follows cliff paths high above the gorge and boasts views that rival any in southern England. Set out before you is Cheddar and the gorge, with panoramic views across the Somerset Levels to Bridgwater Bay and beyond to the Quantocks and Exmoor. The route provides for refreshments and a closer look at Cheddar and the attractions at the halfway stage.

The walk begins in the upper reaches of the gorge below Black Rock nature trail at grid reference 481 545 on the B3135, where parking is available on the road side. Take the West Mendip Way, signposted Draycott, at first climbing steeply through the deciduous woodland to emerge on the higher ground above the gorge. This area above the gorge on the south side is home to the highest inland limestone cliffs in Britain, now a 360-acre nature reserve owned by the Marquess of Bath.

Dramatic views down into the gorge are rivalled by the distant views of the Somerset Levels and the outcrop of Crook Peak.

Across the gorge looking north to the Mendip summit on Black Down.

24

Well-marked paths lead you up through the woodlands below Cheddar Cliffs.

Goats wander the cliffs, helping to keep the scrub under control. They seem friendly enough but have quite a unique aroma.

Continue following the West Mendip Way for a short distance before it heads away from the cliffs, now keeping to the right path that descends gradually along the cliff top. Extreme care is needed on this section as the cliffs are unfenced with a sheer drop to the road some 450ft below. After a mile of exhilarating walking with exceptional views you reach an observation tower above Jacob's Ladder. The ladder is a path of 274 steps leading from the village up the side of the gorge, and are named after a biblical description of a ladder to heaven.

The woodland path now descends to the busy village below. Cheddar is one of Britain's biggest tourist attractions, with an estimated 500,000 visitors per year. It is renowned for its remarkable caves and gorge, but also because of Cheddar cheese. The cheese is famous the world over due to the process of 'cheddaring' which produces a hard, full-flavoured cheese, the original version emanating from Somerset during the 13th century. Once in the village at the foot of the gorge you may want to seek refreshments, visit the attractions or continue at a more leisurely pace crossing the B3135 into The Bays. Take a left turn at Jacobs Cottage, leading you on to Tutors Hill, passing some delightfully named cottages before a path on your right is taken by the side of Appletree Cottage.

The route from here enters National Trust land, with well-marked paths leading up through Cheddar Cliffs. The first part of the climb is extremely steep with no extended views as you are climbing up through a deciduous wooded area. After half a mile the landscape opens up and views start to unfold across the gorge, revealing just how perilous the outward journey was atop the southern cliffs.

On reaching the top of the gorge the path become easy walking over short turfs before it begins to descend. On reaching a ladder stile, turn right to

Pointing the way above Cheddar Cliffs.

The views begin to open up as you emerge from the woodlands.

The limestone grasslands are being regenerated above the gorge with the generous help of National Trust volunteers.

follow the short track back to the road, where a left turn will bring you back to the car parking area. An alternative conclusion to the walk would be to cross the stile, continuing upward and eventually descending via Black Rock.

Exmoor ponies are helping to preserve the ecology of Mendip. They belong to Tawbitts Exmoors of Weddon Cross, a small stud run by two ladies called Jill Langdon and Jackie Ablett who breed Exmoors for conservation grazing throughout the South West and South Wales. They have been running Exmoors on National Trust land since the early 1980s.

The National Trust spends a lot of time and effort removing scrub to restore areas where the grassland has been engulfed, in an attempt to preserve the very rare calcareous limestone grassland that exists on the underlying rock. Bramble, hawthorn, blackthorn, ash, hazel, bracken and gorse have taken over in the decades since grazing was lost from the hills. The agricultural depression in the early 1900s started the exodus of sheep farming from marginal, hard-to-graze areas, allowing the scrub to take over from the huge swathes of open grassland that existed, primarily due to sheep grazing that had continued for hundreds of years. The loss of rabbits in the early 1950s to myxomatosis compounded the problem, and it is in this decade that the scrub really got going. The reinstating of the grassland began in the 1990s, creating a very important habitat for wildflowers and invertebrates, forming the basis for a healthy food chain. The trust manage the scrub and grassland so as to create a 'mosaic' of different habitats, ranging form open grassland through to scrub, scrub woodland and woodland, providing maximum food sources and shelter for birds and mammals.

The trust has 24 volunteers with a group of around eight spending their time on Wednesdays and Fridays every week carrying out practical estate work such as scrub clearing, dry stone walling, footpath clearance, step building, stile and gate building and litter picking. Robert Stephens, the National Trust Warden, told me that volunteers were essential and that they had worked for some 1,300 hours in 2009. The trust always welcomes new people to come along and try their hand.

The views from Burrington Ham encompass Black Down and extend north-west across the Severn Estuary to South Wales.

The Exmoor ponies seen here, a stallion called Golden Treacle and a mare called Alexia, are used for conservation grazing, helping to preserve the ecology of Mendip.

At 1,068ft above sea level, Beacon Batch is the highest point of Mendip.

Black Down is a haven for wildlife with swathes of dense bracken.

Burrington Combe

Just a few miles north-north east of Cheddar Gorge is the second largest dry valley on Mendip, Burrington Combe. Nestling below Mendip's summit at Beacon Batch, Black Down, the combe was created by the same forces as Cheddar Gorge, although not on such a grand scale. The thin soil on the slopes above the combe has created a rich limestone grassland habitat with the warm south-facing slopes a haven for butterflies, while below Black Down, in the sheltered East and West Twin valleys, the more humid microclimate favours ferns and mosses.

At Beacon Batch you reach the highest point of Mendip, the summit of Black Down, 1,068ft above sea level, boasting both ancient and relatively modern sites of historical interest. Beacon Batch is home to ancient Bronze Age barrows but also has a more recent history. A closer look at the summit reveals that it is still littered with mounds, dips and straight lines which were created during World War Two as bombing decoys for the nearby city of Bristol. They were said to look like railway lines and sidings to enemy aircraft. The views north-west from the summit encompass the Severn Estuary and the Welsh coast and on clear days extend further inland to the Brecon Beacons, often seen sporting their winter coat during spells of colder weather.

The trig point confirms the height at 1,068ft.

The heather-clad hillsides and dense bracken provide the perfect habitat for many species of insects and birds. Kestrels and buzzards circle high overhead before diving to catch their prey.

The rowan tree is a feature of upland Britain.

The summit's acidic soil supports a variety of heath-land grasses, with some boggy areas typical of an upland landscape supporting sphagnum mosses and other wetland plants. Black Down is a haven for wildlife, with the swathes of heather and dense bracken providing the perfect habitat for many species of insects and birds. Kestrels and buzzards circle high overhead before diving to catch their prey. The upper slopes of the ridge at Black Down are home to occasional solitary trees, creating a unique Mendip landscape. The rowan tree is a feature of upland Britain, growing to a higher altitude than any other species, and several examples can be found on Black Down. The rowan's wood is strong and flexible, and was ideal for making bows in the Middle Ages. The wood was also often used for carving and for traditional tool handles, spindles and spinning wheels, as well as walking sticks. The flowers blossom in the early summer and once fertilised develop into bright red berries during August to September. The berries are an excellent source of food for the wild birds, but they can be used for a variety of other purposes including wine-making and rowan berry jelly.

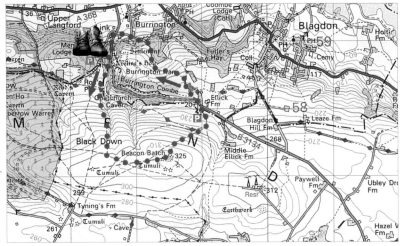

Mendip Summit Walk

Distance: 4 miles with an estimated time of 2–2.5 hours.

This is an exhilarating walk from beneath the limestone cliffs of Burrington to Mendip's highest point, Beacon Batch, 1,068ft above sea level. The walk does require an initial steep climb of 700ft to reach Black Down just under a mile from the start. It continues over relatively level ground to reach Beacon Batch trig point, before a steady descent back to Burrington. The walk begins at grid reference 476 588 at the car park in Burrington Combe.

Perhaps the most famous visitor to spend the night at Burrington Combe was Revd Augustus Montague Toplady, who in 1763, as tradition has it, sheltered from a thunderstorm in the cleft in the limestone rock. His experience inspired him to write the words to the well-known hymn *Rock of Ages*.

In 1763 Revd Augustus Montague Toplady was inspired to write the words to the well known hymn *Rock of Ages* while sheltering in the cleft here at Burrington Combe.

The heather-clad slopes are a delight any time of year.

The views from Black Down looking west encompass Brean Down and the island of Steep Holme, rising almost 250ft from the seabed some 18 miles distant.

From the car park cross the B3134 to the Rock of Ages, following the roadside path up toward Aveline's Hole, where a track on your right leads up West Twin valley, beginning the steep ascent to Black Down.

The route initially follows the river bed of West Twin brook, is rocky underfoot and can be wet in times of heavy rainfall, so strong walking boots are essential. Beyond a spring the route becomes steeper as you enter the open ground of Black Down, with its heather-clad slopes a delight when in full bloom. Several paths lead off from the route, but continue forward with West Twin on your left. Just under a mile from the start of the walk you come across a meeting of paths high on the top of Black Down. Turn left, following clear paths to the triangulation pillar at Beacon Batch.

Several small mounds can be seen straddling the straight paths atop Black Down. These were created during World War Two as bombing decoys to protect the nearby city of Bristol.

The magnificent views continue north across the Severn Estuary to the snow-capped mountains of Wales.

From the summit of Mendip the route now begins its descent back to Burrington, taking the left path, providing distant views to the Welsh coast and the Brecon Beacons and, somewhat closer to home, Blagdon and Chew Valley lakes, with occasional aircraft spotted arriving and departing from Bristol International Airport.

On reaching the B3134 head left to a parking area where a path leads off behind the car park left toward Burrington. Follow this path across Burrington Ham, an open area of limestone grassland with excellent views back toward Black Down. Continue on the path, ignoring the first left fork to where the track begins descending through a woodland to emerge on a bridleway, eventually reaching a quiet lane. Turn left following Ham Link Lane back to the B3134, where another left turn will eventually bring you back to the car park in Burrington Combe.

The warmth of a late September day adds to the pleasure of a walk on Mendip, augmented by the autumnal colouration here on Burrington Ham.

Looking back towards Black Down from the B3134. Threatening skies are highlighted by the winter sun and bring the promise of winter storms.

Charterhouse

A short distance from the hamlet of Charterhouse, a mile south-east of Black Down, is the old Charterhouse School. It is now used as an outdoor centre catering for schools and colleges, with a wide variety of outdoor activities on offer including caving, rock climbing and navigation skills, and it even boasts its own observatory in the grounds. The original Victorian school closed its doors in 1946 but soon began to be used as a centre for groups coming to explore Mendip. Those early visitors slept in the hall. During the mid-1960s wooden cabins were built to improve the accommodation and these were comfortable and dry, a vast improvement on the early days. As with most things standards improved, and 2004 saw the cabins replaced by an award-winning build incorporating green technologies.

The whitewashed school buildings reflect the warm summer sun high upon the Mendip plateau, with the sign confirming that Charterhouse in is an Area of Outstanding Natural Beauty. The bright red postbox must have seen countless cards and letters passing through to the folks back home, telling plentiful tales of adventures in the hills. The cipher on the postbox indicates that it was installed after 1952.

St Hugh's Church, close to the hamlet of Charterhouse.

The Church of St Hugh, close to the hamlet of Charterhouse, was built in 1909 to serve the miners of Charterhouse, taking its name from Hugh of Avalon, a Carthusian monk. The church was built on the site of a miners' welfare hall as an addition to the original building. Prior to 1909 Charterhouse School was used for baptisms, with the original portable font from the school now serving as the font in the present church.

The commanding cross in the churchyard dates from 1909.

'Gruffy ground' close to Charterhouse, immersed in a warm glow from the subtle light of late evening summer sun.

Velvet Bottom Walk

Distance: 5 miles with an estimated time of 2–2.5 hours.

This delightful walk begins at the end of a 'no through road', leading off the minor crossroads at Charterhouse. If travelling from the B3134 take the left turn at the crossroads by the post box to arrive at grid reference 505 557. The walk takes in quiet country lanes and dry limestone valleys.

The walk begins following the footpath to your left, heading north. A gravel track continues through 'gruffy ground', the local name for the scarred landscape of the former lead workings. The area was occupied by the Romans to exploit the lead deposits, although it has been suggested lead was mined from earlier times. Evidence of a small Roman fort has been found dating from the first century, with further excavations revealing that smelting was carried out on the site. The lead would have been transported along the minor roads, later linking up with the Fosse Way.

The area close to Charterhouse School was once the site of a Roman fort, with the 'gruffy ground' revealing its history as an important lead-mining area.

High summer produces warm hues for the backdrop of this fine thistle growing near to Ubley Warren.

The open countryside is a delight to walk with several encounters on the way.

An amphitheatre has been discovered west of the main settlement, being the only one in England associated with a lead mine, emphasising the importance of the area to the Romans. Surveyed in 1909, it is believed to have been a place of entertainment for the soldiers at the Roman fort. The track emerges on to the Charterhouse road where you turn left for a short distance back to the minor crossroads before turning right, signposted Shipham. Easy walking on the unclassified lane for one and a half miles will bring you to a drive on your left.

As late summer gradually begins to slip away the bracken and grasslands transform into a wonderful display of autumnal hues.

Close to the road at Charterhouse looking back to Velvet Bottom, a unique habitat for adders and lizards.

Follow the drive to the right of Charterhouse Farm, heading uphill toward Piney Sleigh Farm. At the cattle grid turn left, taking the course of the West Mendip Way. The long-distance path crosses the field for half a mile before entering Long Wood. Continue through the woodland, heading downhill to emerge in the dry valley of Black Rock. Cross a stone stile on your left, leaving the West Mendip Way to follow the path up through Velvet Bottom for just over a mile to reach the Charterhouse road.

The gruffy ground reveals the extent of the lead mining that has taken place over centuries in the dry valley. Take care as the dry valley is a perfect habitat for adders. Turn right onto the minor road and in a short distance take the gate on your left to continue on a path that leads back to the parking area.

Gruffy ground, Ubley Warren. It is now a nature reserve purchased in 1989 from Bristol University, forming part of the Cheddar Gorge Site of Special Scientific Interest (SSSI).

The grass in the foreground seems to appear gold in the late summer sun, but it was only lead that was found here at Velvet Bottom. You may just spot the signpost under the tree that points the way of a path that continues on through to Black Rock, eventually emerging above Cheddar Gorge, a distance of some three miles.

Lead was last mined at Velvet Bottom, a dry limestone valley, in 1908 when the Victorians ceased a tradition that had begun before Roman times. The buddle pits that were used for separating the ore and slag can still be distinguished, as can the series of dams and settling beds further down the valley. Purchased from Bristol Water in 1999, Velvet Bottom forms part of the Cheddar Gorge SSSI along with nearby Ubley Warren. The path through Velvet Bottom eventually emerges above Cheddar Gorge, a distance of some three miles.

An old water pump, Charterhouse. It is a simple design, thought to have originated in China thousands of years ago. An endless chain with a series of circular discs attached is run through water. As the chain runs up a pipe with a diameter slightly larger than the discs water is drawn up, trapped and then dispersed at the top.

A bitter cold spell high on Mendip can make travel difficult but creates a contrasting scene.

Priddy Mineries lie just over 850ft above sea level.

Priddy Mineries

A short distance east from Charterhouse the evidence of mining continues, and archaeologists have made discoveries around Priddy dating back over 35,000 years. These include evidence of Bronze Age activity and the Priddy Circles, which suggest the area was once home to a large number of people. The circles have proved to be rather mystifying and their exact use remains a topic of debate. One theory suggests that they were building projects abandoned because the area was unstable, while another claims they may have been for ceremonial use, but differing from stone circles. Lead-working close to Priddy dates back to Roman times, and theories suggest that the extensive lead mines would have been an influential factor in the Roman invasion, as lead was valuable to the Roman Empire. Today, Priddy Pools, St Cuthberts and Chewton Mineries, known as Priddy Mineries, are a nature reserve, rich in a variety of flora and fauna with dragonflies and newts abundant. The area has a high concentration of lead, particularly around the old spoil heaps.

Opposite: The pools create a mysterious atmosphere, reflecting the partially-clouded summer skies.

The plateau is home to an infinite variety of wild flowers, including white campion.

This sheltered dry stone wall provides a haven for mosses.

Dry stone walls are a traditional feature of the rural landscape of the scattered farms and settlements of the western plateau. Mendip is criss-crossed by a labyrinth of quiet country lanes. Some connect villages by seemingly the shortest route, while others meander to isolated farming communities. Here on the higher plateau the patchwork of fields is bordered by sparse, exposed, wind-blown hedgerows amid the dry stone walls, while further east you will find the quintessentially English quiet and leafy country lanes. The main agricultural feature of the western plateau is pastureland divided by the prominent stone walls. The majority of the pastures remain much as they would have been at the turn of the 20th century, unaffected by the need to accommodate modern farming methods by removing hedgerows to create larger fields, as is more common the further east you travel. The steeper southern slopes of western Mendip are classed as unimproved limestone grasslands and are now important conservation areas. A few conifer plantations have been grown on the western plateau, whereas the eastern slopes are home to broad-leafed woodlands, particularly in the valleys.

Winter sun highlighting the patchwork of stone enclosures against a background of mounting skies, helping to create an almost surreal atmosphere.

Agriculture plays an important role in the Mendips. High up on the plateau the air is filled with dust from the harvesting on a glorious dry summer day.

A friendly pair pose for the camera while most of the herd seem content to take advantage of the warm summer sun.

The Mendip landscape began to change to its present state during the later part of the 18th century when the traditional sheep walks were enclosed by dry stone walls and hedges. The influence of the Romans is clear to see, with the straight lines of some roads that transverse the western plateau contrasting greatly with the winding country lanes of eastern Mendip. Local legend has it that the words of *Jerusalem,* written by William Blake, were describing the Mendips as the 'mountains green' and Priddy as the 'dark satanic mills'.

Some things have to be done. Essential duties include muckspreading to ensure a good growth of grass for the following spring. I did ensure that I was not downwind at the time.

Waldegrave Pool, one of many pools with an historic connection to past lead-mining activities, high on the Mendip plateau. The icy grip of a December morning is beginning to take a hold on the pool, with the promise of snow from the mounting clouds.

50

Several factors contributed to the closure of the lead-mining industry, one being the rapidly falling price of imported lead, and another the pollution of the water supply at Wookey Hole. The pools on Priddy were used for washing the ore, and the waste water drained underground. Subsequent tests proved that the polluted water eventually re-emerged at Wookey Hole Paper Mill.

Sedges are to be found growing at the periphery of the pools, providing a haven for wildlife including newts, frogs and toads.

The area close to Priddy known as North Hill lies over 850ft above sea level and bears witness to some of the harshest winter weather on Mendip.

The remnants of a distant summer now taking on a new pose in the grip of midwinter.

Winter's icy grip begins to take hold.

Priddy

Priddy is a village set high up in the Mendip Hills, sometimes described as bleak in the most pleasant sense of the word during the midwinter, but alive in the summer. July sees the village hold what is described as the friendliest folk festival in England, while August heralds the arrival of thousands of visitors for the traditional Sheep Fair.

A notice on the green states that: 'These hurdles are a symbolic reconstruction of the original collection which were stored here to form the pens for the Sheep Fair which moved from Wells to Priddy in 1348 at the outbreak of the black death.'

A local legend says that as long as the hurdle stack remains in the village then so will the fair.

The postbox in the village bears the cipher GR VI, dating the box to the reign of King George VI (1936–52).

The ash hurdles, symbolic of the annual sheep fair, are no longer used to pen the sheep but are still an integral part of village folklore.

A well-built stile provides easy access over the dry stone wall.

The pens that hold the sheep for auction today are a far cry from the traditional wooden hurdles of yesteryear, but they do the job. The fair is not only about sheep, but they are the main focus of the day. This fine-looking flock seem very inquisitive.

Priddy Sheep Fair

Originally held on 10 August to mark the feast of St Lawrence the Martyr, the Sheep Fair is now held annually on the nearest Wednesday to 21 August. There is evidence to suggest that a fair was held at Priddy long before 1348, perhaps as a far back as Iron Age times, when the village's population was thought to be far greater than it is today. Farmers and families alike gather at Priddy for the West Country's most historic annual sheep fair. The event attracts traditional horse sellers and sheep dealers to the auctions held on the green, and thousands of visitors travel to the remote village high on the Mendip plateau to witness sheep shearing displays and craftsmen demonstrating skills that can be traced back centuries. A traditional fun fair and stalls complete the scene.

Sheep Fair number 661 took place on a hot summer's day in August 2009, with a record number of sheep entered.

Traditional crafts, a fun fair and live entertainment can all be found at Priddy Sheep Fair.

Livestock trading is still the mainstay of the event, much as it would have been in 1348.

Priddy plays host to the traditional Boxing Day Hunt. The winter weather sets the perfect mood, with blue skies contrasting vividly with the traditional red jackets of the hunt masters. As the riders, horses and hounds prepare, the green provides the perfect location for a chat before the off.

Priddy is also the centre of attention outside the warmer summer months as it is the home of the traditional Boxing Day Hunt, attracting large crowds on the green to view the colourful, quintessentially rural scene and to meet with old friends. The origins of hunting in Mendip can be traced back as far as 1760. The Mendip Hunt, as it is known today, was formed in 1940. Hunting begins in November running through until March, with the hunt covering an area as far south as the Somerset Levels and north to the outskirts of Bath. The hunt has three masters and a strong following, meeting twice a week during the season.

A closer inspection of one of the most colourful events in the countryside.

They're off! – at great speed, first the hounds and then the hunt master.

Ebbor Gorge Walk

Distance: 7 miles with an estimated time of 3.5–4 hours.

Ebbor Gorge nature reserve lies just off Pelting Drove, the single-track road from Priddy to Wookey Hole. The walk to Priddy begins from the car park at Ebbor Gorge, grid reference 520 485, taking the trail through the gorge before emerging on to open ground following well-worn paths across North Hill. Easy walking on quiet country lanes on the return journey allows for a well-earned rest at Priddy. The gorge is owned by the National Trust and run by English Nature. An alternative first part of the route, avoiding a steep section, can be taken using the path above the gorge, as the route up through the gorge contains a very steep section that requires agility and can be very slippery. Stout footwear is advisable for this walk.

Follow the main path that is well marked (red arrow) from the car park, initially descending then climbing up through the dry limestone gorge carved by a river that has long since disappeared. The ancient wooded slopes and limestone cliffs have revealed bones of mammals dating from the last Ice Age found in two caves that are said to have provided shelter to Neolithic man in around 3000 BC.

The route up through the dry limestone gorge requires a degree of agility.

This life-size bear greats you as you descend into the gorge.

Ebbor Gorge is owned by the National Trust and run by English Nature.

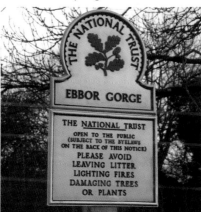

Once above the gorge the route turns left to join the West Mendip Way. Once you have emerged from the woodland take a look back, as you are rewarded with spectacular views of the Somerset Levels and further west to the Quantocks and Exmoor. At the top of the next field the path leaves the West Mendip Way, taking a curve to the right and heading towards the transmitter mast at Pen Hill. After a short distance an iron stile on your left takes you onto the Monarch's Way for the next mile, following the wall before reaching the Wells Road. The Monarch's Way is a long-distance footpath based on the route taken by King Charles II after defeat by Cromwell at the battle of Worcester in 1651. Turn right onto the road and in a short distance take the path on your left to Priddy Pools. After 500 yards leave the Monarch's Way to take the left fork, beginning the ascent of North Hill keeping the stone wall on your left passing Priddy Nine Barrows.

Winter sun highlights the wetland grasses around Priddy Pools.

Go through the gate to follow the path across the field to Ashen Hill Barrows, a group of eight barrows running west to east, sometimes mistaken for Priddy Nine Barrows. From here head south-west to descend to Nine Barrows Lane. Turn left to follow the lane, turning left again at the minor junction at Priddy. Follow the lane down hill to the green at Priddy, where a well-deserved rest and refreshment can be taken at one of the two village pubs.

Priddy Nine Barrows are a prominent feature on the ridge of North Hill and date back over 4,000 years to the Bronze Age. The barrows consist of a row of seven, with a further two separated from main group.

A well-deserved rest can be had at one of two pubs in Priddy. Somerset is renowned for its cider and it is celebrated here at the 15th-century New Inn.

The return to Ebbor is a straightforward amble taking Pelting Drove, a blue single-track road with passing places, signs pointing the way. The lane undulates across the limestone plateau for a mile before dropping down steeply to the car park at Ebbor Gorge. The views across the Somerset Levels on reaching the area known as Deer Leap on this last leg of the walk are truly breathtaking.

Deer Leap. The views that open up as the lane begins to descend the southern slopes of Mendip are awe-inspiring. The panorama south-west across the Somerset Levels to Bridgwater Bay encompasses the Quantock Hills and distant Exmoor, seen here under a blanket of snow.

The icy cold mists of a winter morning can craft intriguing, sometimes surreal landscapes.

Leaving Ebbor Gorge we continue eastward, where we come across the most notable modern-day man-made feature by far on Mendip, the Mendip transmitter. Sited at Pen Hill, 1,000ft above sea level, the transmitter was originally built by the BBC as a BBC 2 transmitter, with construction beginning in 1967. The first transmission followed in December 1969. The structure is a cylindrical tower rising 920ft into the Somerset skyline.

Frosted remains of the past summer's hedgerow.

A dusting of snow serves to highlight the two-arch pedestrian bridge and ford close to the source of the river at Dumpers Lane, Chewton Mendip.

The Chew Valley

From Pen Hill we head north-east to the village of Chewton Mendip, where the River Chew rises from two springs fed by rainwater draining from Chew Down, close to Ston Easton. At Chewton Mendip we see the first clear signs of the river, where a somewhat bland outlet heralds the young river's arrival, while a rather attractive double-arched bridge provides pedestrian access over a ford close to the centre of the village at Dumpers Lane.

Above the River Chew at Ford the heavy snow conjures up a Christmas card scene.

This delightful stone crossing is to be found at Ford. The river provides a picturesque scene as it meanders on the first part of its journey, enhanced by the stillness about its banks of a cold winter's morning.

The upper reaches of the river are shallow and at times fast-flowing. The Chew meanders for 1.5 miles through the small settlement at Ford to reach Litton, where the river enters two reservoirs built over a century ago to supply Bristol with drinking water. These were the predecessors of Chew Valley Lake, which nestles in the foothills of the Mendips. Beyond Litton the river continues north-west through the Somerset countryside, joined on its meandering journey by several small tributaries, perhaps most notably one that rises high in the hills close to Priddy before flowing into the reservoir.

The waterfall creates a refreshing scene, with a thin veil of mist covering the surface of the water and the low winter sun slowly regaining the upper hand against the icy cold of a winter's morning.

Autumn is one of the best times to visit Chew Valley Lake, with several thousand wildfowl present. The lake also supports a variety of waders, gulls and other occasional rare visitors which are an added attraction for the numerous birdwatchers.

Chew Valley Lake was created to meet the need to increase the drinking water supply to the rapidly developing city of Bristol. Plans were put forward to construct the reservoir as early as 1939 and an Act of Parliament was passed but put on hold because of World War Two. To enable the construction and the flooding of the once rich farmland, many farmsteads and houses had to be demolished. Work eventually began in 1950, with the official opening by Queen Elizabeth II on 17 April 1956. At times of drought the level of water falls to reveal hedgerows, trees and the old road bridge. Chew Valley Lake nestles in the northern foothills of the Mendips at the lowest part of the Chew Valley. The statistics for the lake reveal the capacity to be 4,500 million gallons, making the lake the largest man-made freshwater lake in the south-west of England. Although opened in 1956, it was not until February 1958 that it first reached its full capacity.

One remarkable fact is that the maximum depth of the lake, when filled to capacity, is a mere 37ft, with an average depth of just 14ft. The lake rose 19 inches in 12 hours as a result of the extremely heavy rains of 1968 that devastated much of Mendip, including Cheddar Gorge. The alarm was sounded warning that the dam might not hold and evacuations were carried out downstream as a precaution, although fortunately it was a false alarm.

The lake is an important site for wintering birds and 285 species have been recorded. Designated a Site of Special Scientific Interest (SSSI), the lake has a sound future with the majority of the area around falling under the Mendip Hills Area of Outstanding Natural Beauty (AONB).

During long periods of dry weather the water level falls to reveal old hedgerows, tree stumps and the old road bridge.

Low light across the lake side. The autumn hues of the trees are in striking contrast to the gloomy skies and the cool waters of the lake. The periphery of the lake is a crucial habitat for wintering wildfowl and resident birds alike, with the area designated a Site of Special Scientific Interest (SSSI).

Looking back to the hills from Herons Green.

The lake provides the perfect habitat for resident and visiting swans. There seems to be some debate as to whether Mute swans pair for life or just for one season, but there is no doubt that established pairs breed more successfully.

Mute swans begin their nest-building in March. The male swan (the cob) collects the nesting material while the female (the pen) builds the nest. The male watches over the female on the nest never far away and will hiss and flap at any intruders. Although called mute they are not silent birds, and it is true that the flapping wings of a swan can break a human's arm. The female lays up to eight eggs, which hatch after 36 days. The cygnets will remain with their parents until the following winter, by then starting to lose their distinctive grey and brown feathers, although taking a full year or more before sporting a full white coat. It will be a further two years before the cygnets are ready to breed. Their main source of food is underwater plants and grasses which are found in abundance on the lake's edge. The Mute swan is the only resident swan in Britain, although it is joined by Whooper and Bewick's swans during the winter months. The Mute swan has played a leading role in man's literary development as the flight feathers were once used as quill pens, later to be known as just pens, taking their name from the female swan.

Cygnets are grey but they develop brown feathers which they keep over winter until their second year.

A glorious panorama of the lake on a beautiful winter's day. The sailing rights to Chew Valley Lake are leased to Chew Valley Lake Sailing Club.

Sailing boats on the lake.

Part Two:
Eastern Mendip

Maesbury Castle

Overlooking the southern flanks of Mendip high above the village of Croscombe is the ancient site of Maesbury Iron Age hill fort. The site offers almost a 360-degree panorama, a unique view from the Mendip escarpment. The remains of the earthworks, like those at any ancient site, are best viewed from the air, but a close inspection of the top of the hill and a little imagination leaves one in no doubt that it must have once been a safe place to live. Maesbury Castle had a single rampart up to 18ft high with a second outer ditch. On the northern section the remains of a moat can be seen and during wet spells it is subject to flooding, recreating the original feature.

On top of the rampart looking west on the southern edge of the hill fort.

A moat is believed to have existed below the northern sections of the rampart and the outer ditch. This view after a spell of wet weather clearly shows what it might have looked like when first constructed. The steep slopes on this north-western section are in deep shade from the winter sun.

Gorse and bracken are now prevalent on the northern section of the rampart, adding to the rugged, remote feel to this area of the Mendip Hills.

Looking back northwards to the first giant wind turbine on Mendip at Shooters Bottom. Local place names have always held a deep fascination and are the subject of great debate. Many a small boy must have come up with a theory about its origin. The unrivalled vista from the hill fort location would have been uninterrupted before the trees grew on the north-western slopes over the last century.

Without doubt the finest views from Maesbury Castle are southwards to the ancient Isle of Avalon and Glastonbury Tor, a distinctive landmark rising from the Somerset Levels. The mist adds to the mystique.

A close look at the gorse in winter reveals that the seeds are ripening ready for dispersal, in great contrast to the plant in prolific bloom with its display of vivid yellow flowers from spring onwards. Depending on the mildness of the seasons gorse will sometimes burst into sporadic flower in winter.

The traditional boat house is still surviving, with the platforms along the edge of the lake used as fishing stations.

Emborough

We have now crossed the divide between western and eastern Mendip, leaving behind the exposed limestone outcrops and dry stone walls to find a broad-leafed woodland enhancing the setting for Emborough Pond, known locally as Lechmere Water. Originally a small mill pond, the lake was created by Capability Brown with a dam built at its eastern end. The pond today covers an area exceeding 10 acres, but it is still referred to locally and on maps as a pond, reflecting it early origins. It is now a popular destination for anglers, with platforms used as fishing bays built around the pond's woodland edge. It is from here that a small stream runs underground, emerging at Blackers Hill where a river's journey begins, meandering generally eastwards through the Nettlebridge and then Wadbury Valley, where its importance to past industrial activity can not be underestimated. Coal measures are exposed at the surface close to the pond, but were never productive unlike those a few miles further east in the villages of Chilcompton and Holcombe.

As autumn approaches the patchwork of fields and labyrinth of Mendip lanes become a hive of activity from early morning till late evening, with farmers busy gathering in the crops. The sunlight from a beautiful summer's evening here at Emborough drenches the whole scene in a glorious warm glow.

The first large-scale wind turbine on Mendip somehow seems to complement the evening sky at sunset.

The Mendip Hills are rich in agricultural diversity and remain an important working environment.

Another modern-day addition a mile or so from Emborough Pond is the first large-scale wind turbine on Mendip. The turbine was erected and began producing electricity in 2008 at Shooters Bottom, close to Chewton Mendip. The structure rises over 200ft into the Mendip sky, being conspicuous from a far distance, but is said to produce enough electricity for 2,000 homes per year.

Snow, frost and the low winter sun creates a captivating scene here at Emborough.

The summer sun envelopes the church in a warm glow. The shape and location of the Blessed Virgin Mary suggest that it dates from Saxon times.

The name Emborough is thought to derive from the name for a 'smooth hill', and the village is home to the parish church of the Blessed Virgin Mary, which provides commanding views over the surrounding countryside to Chewton Mendip and beyond. It is a simple stone structure dating from mediaeval times, having been extensively renovated during the 18th century. The site may have been a place of worship in Saxon times. The central tower has a 13th-century base rising to an elegant parapet with pinnacles at each corner. It is now cared for by the Churches Conservation Trust. The other church in their care on Mendip is further east at Holcombe.

Peace and tranquillity on the frozen waters of the lake.

The freezing combination of snow and ice can bring early morning mists
that create eerie scenes as the low winter sun begins to burn through.

The serenity of the boat house is enhanced by the stillness of the frozen lake. It is said that a
car was driven on the frozen waters during the severe winter of 1963.

Some of the tunnels and bridges still remain. This one at Chilcompton is a distant reminder of the halcyon days of steam.

Chilcompton

In 1870 plans were put forward by the Somerset & Dorset Railway to build an extension from the existing line at Evercreech Junction over the Mendip Hills to Bath. The construction was by no means an easy task, as the route would have to follow the contours of the hills to climb above 800ft to the summit at Maesbury (spelt 'Masbury' by the railway), creating many twists and turns along the way. Once completed it would create a link from the Midlands via Bath to the south coast. Numerous rock cuttings, embankments, tunnels and bridges had to be created along the 26-mile route.

Work began in 1872, with the first passenger service commencing in July 1874. Trains making the ascent over the Mendips had to overcome gradients of 1 in 50, sometimes necessitating what were known as double-headers. Two locomotives were used to haul some of the heavy passenger trains from Radstock to Masbury summit before beginning the descent into Shepton Mallet. At Evercreech Junction one would uncouple, returning to Radstock, while the other continued the journey south, leaving the Mendip Hills behind.

The line eventually closed in March 1966, as a consequence of the Beeching axe, with much of the infrastructure dismantled in the late 1960s. However, many of the tunnels and bridges can still be seen today, a distant reminder of the halcyon days of steam on the Somerset & Dorset Railway, often affectionately known as the Slow & Dirty.

To mark the 25th anniversary of the closure of the line, church bells were rung in the villages that had built up a strong, affectionate relationship and dependency on the line during its 92 years of service. The line ran above a Mendip valley here at Chilcompton on its journey through rock cuttings and tunnels on the steep climb south from Radstock to Binegar. The Somerset & Dorset Railway Heritage Trust, based at Midsomer Norton South Station, just two miles north from Chilcompton, has plans to once again run steam trains south towards Chilcompton. Track-laying is well underway from the restored Midsomer Norton Station, edging steadily closer to the Chilcompton Tunnels.

Plans are underway to re-lay the track from Midsomer Norton to bring steam trains back to the abandoned station here at Chilcompton.

The sheltered valley runs east to west, with frosts lingering on the shaded north-facing slopes. The valley floor is never warmed by the low winter sun.

Agricultural machinery that was once cutting-edge technology but is now no longer required is left to the unforgiving elements and rampant vegetation.

The valley at Chilcompton was once home to a thriving watercress business fed by the natural springs close to the valley floor. As a result of pig farming in the 1960s and 1970s the northern slopes of the valley became bare soil, but have returned to deciduous woodland and in places are overgrown with ivy and brambles. In earlier times the stream would have been utilised as a means of power for milling. The small stream still tumbles along the valley floor on its journey through to the lower part of the village.

There are several theories about the village's name and it is often thought to be associated with cold, 'chill', and 'combe' or 'compton' meaning 'valley', as the original part of village is situated in the valley close to St John's Church. The close proximity of the Fosse Way at Stratton would almost certainly have involved Roman occupation at some time. Chilcompton has a mention in the *Domesday Book*, completed in 1086.

Brambles soon take hold if unchecked, but produce delicious late summer fruits, followed by a wonderful display of colour from their autumn leaves.

Chilcompton, like most of Mendip, has a plethora of footpaths.

North of Chilcompton the long-abandoned Somerset & Dorset Railway had to travel through a deep rock cutting, and still required a tunnel crossed by a quiet country lane that descends steeply to the lower part of the village. The area, like most of Mendip, has a plethora of footpaths linking the extended village that clings to the contours of the hillside. In contrast to the stone-wall enclosures of western Mendip, hedgerows are a more common feature and in late summer are abundant with blackberries and bright red hips. The hips are the fruit of the dog rose, and inside are fibrous seeds that are highly irritant, bringing back childhood memories of dropping the contents of hips down each other's necks. As a result, the seeds were nicknamed 'hitching powders'.

The beautiful serene hues of autumnal colour begin to appear with the haw. The fruit of the hawthorn is more crimson and spherical than its closely associated hip. In mediaeval times the hawthorn was said to protect houses from evil spirits.

Rebuilt in 1839, St John's Church retains its original tower, thought to date from the prosperous 15th century. It is a rather splendid church set in a characteristic Mendip valley.

World War Two claimed the lives of 16 brave men from Chilcompton, a tremendous loss for a small village. On Bowden Hill, as in every village and town throughout Britain, they are not forgotten and poppies are laid on Remembrance Sunday. The Cornish granite cross was originally erected in 1921 to honour the fallen of World War One.

The granite cross commemorating the fallen of two World Wars stands proudly on the hillside overlooking the older part of the village.

A tranquil setting for a footpath that runs as a companion to the small stream, veiled with dappled late summer sunlight reflecting on the water, as it flows through the Pitching Chilcompton.

The stream that runs through the valley continues its journey in a tranquil setting in the lower part of the village known as The Pitching, where a footpath follows its course, linking the old Church House to the church. Church House was built entirely by volunteers in the early 1900s and was used extensively by the church and the old infants' school alike until closure in the late 1990s. St John's Church was rebuilt in 1839, retaining the impressive tower dating from 1460. The small stream continues its meandering journey, soon leaving behind the Mendips to later emerge further north as the River Somer, its source just over two miles south-west, close to Old Down, Emborough.

Opposite: The subtle light of a late summer's evening creates a captivating scene at Chilcompton, the double-arch bridge reflected in the meandering stream.

The clear waters create interesting light and textures as they ripple over the undisturbed shallow river bed.

A reminder of earlier days with the refurbished Midland Mark I SK coach.

Somerset & Dorset Railway Heritage Trust

Just two miles north from Chilcompton is to be found the site of the next station on the line towards Bath – Midsomer Norton South. Here you will find the home of the Somerset & Dorset Railway Heritage Trust, which is now bringing the memories of steam back to life with the S&D Mendip Main Line Project. Since 1996 work has been ongoing by a dedicated group of volunteers to restore the old

station buildings and re-lay a section of track southwards, with the aim to run steam trains once again from Midsomer Norton towards Chilcompton. The line will provide not only a nostalgic train journey, but also a most picturesque one, as it follows a course cut into the hillside overlooking a rural Mendip valley.

Midsomer Norton South Station, as it says, lies to the south of Midsomer Norton, high above the town in the foothills of Mendip. It was from nearby Radstock that the serious climb over the Mendip Hills began, culminating at Masbury as we have already noted, before descending steeply to Shepton Mallet. From Radstock, the ruling gradient is 1 in 50, and shortly after the platform at Midsomer Norton the gradient becomes 1 in 53, a considerable climb for a steam locomotive and even more so from a standing start at the station.

The station buildings, goods shed, stable block and wartime pillbox have all been lovingly

A close look at a freight wagon ready to roll.

restored, recreating a bygone era. The signal box is being rebuilt down to the last detail, with the levers and instruments due to be fully connected to signals and points in working order, possibly in time for the return of passenger traffic. The signalman would have other duties, and here at Midsomer Norton it was the greenhouse next to the signal box that kept him busy during a day's work. This is now also being fully rebuilt. Midsomer Norton won the best-kept station award for several years, not least due to its magnificent floral displays throughout the summer months, helped by the work in the greenhouse.

The project has a diesel shunter, a Sentinel 0-4-0 vertical-boiler steam locomotive, under restoration, freight and passenger rolling stock and a static buffet coach that is used as was intended (although it is not mobile) for refreshments. Completion of additional track-laying, together with the necessary safety works and inspections, could see the return of a public passenger service in 2010.

The signal box has been sympathetically rebuilt to the original design, with the brasswork shining as it would have done back in the halcyon days of steam.

Looking back to the station from the restored track. A severe frost highlights the wooden sleepers.

The Trust aims to restore the track towards Chilcompton and then maybe in the longer term reach Shepton Mallet in one direction and Radstock in the other. Perhaps the most famous locomotive to have seen service on the Somerset & Dorset was 9F 2-10-0 No.92220 *Evening Star*. It was in September 1962 that it pulled the last 'Pines Express' – a daily Manchester to Bournemouth service – over the Mendip Hills without assistance.

A familiar sight in Somerset, a reminder of World War Two, is the pillbox, with one located overlooking the station at Midsomer Norton and the next in line standing above Chilcompton Tunnels, north of Chilcompton. When the invasion of the Channel Islands took place, leaving Britain more vulnerable, a plan was devised to construct defensive lines in the county, known as CHQ lines, or stop lines. A line ran east from Bridgwater to Freshford, known as the Green Line, having a total of 107 boxes. Construction began in 1940 and by 1941, when building ceased, over 1,000 pillboxes were in place. The pillbox would not have been manned on a permanent basis but would have been used by the Home Guard.

Fish plates used to connect the rails.

The pillbox overlooking the station forms part of the new museum, mainly located in the old stable block, next to which it is planned to recreate a scene from the 1940s, complete with an Anderson shelter. Located in the pillbox is a most fascinating collection of war memorabilia, displayed for visitors to see. The museum will not only provide an insight to what life would have been like on the Somerset & Dorset Railway, but also a look back at life in the war years of the late 1930s through to the early 1940s.

The fascinating collection of war memorabilia is aptly displayed in the original pillbox.

The Nettlebridge Valley from Downside, south of Chilcompton.

Nettlebridge Valley and Stratton-on-the-Fosse

The villages of eastern Mendip support the highest populations of the region and are generally larger than those on the western plateau, but they still retain a scattered feel, most with a rich historical heritage and steeped in folklore. The mellow villages of eastern Mendip were traditionally built from a variety of local stone ranging from Oolite, described as honey-coloured, to White Lias and grey Doulting stone. The villages of eastern Mendip are well documented for their fine church towers, some clearly visible, while others are hidden in sheltered valleys, providing a safe haven for the ancient villages in disturbed times. The long tradition of mining in Mendip, with the legacy of lead and the gruffy ground we left behind on the higher plateau, was subsequently continued eastward in the Nettlebridge Valley and the villages of Chilcompton and Holcombe. A rich seam of black gold was discovered that shaped the landscape of eastern Mendip in the 19th century, with production continuing right up until the 1970s. Coal was initially mined just below and sometimes on the surface on a small scale within the Nettlebridge Valley, but during the late 19th century deeper large-scale mines were sunk at Chilcompton and a little north of Kilmersdon at Haydon. With its long association with mining it has been suggested that the name Mendip comes from the medieval 'myne deepes'.

Moorewood Colliery, near to Gurney Slade, was the most westerly deep mine on Mendip, begun in 1824 with production ceasing in 1873 due to flooding, which was the reason for several Mendip coal mine closures. In 1910 the mine was reopened with a connection to the Somerset & Dorset Railway close to Chilcompton. Production continued but it never achieved a good profit and finally closed in 1923.

The deepest mine in Somerset was sunk at Strap Pit Downside, reaching a depth of 1,838ft in 1862. The mine was temporarily closed then reopened as part of the Somerset coalfield in 1953. Nearby Chilcompton New Rock Colliery, first sunk in 1816, had been taken into new ownership, forming part of the Somerset coalfield. During their heyday the mines employed upwards of 700 men. In 1947 the National Coal Board (NCB) took over the mines forming the Mendip Colliery. The mines were in full operation by 1964, but despite the labour force being increased, with the arrival of several mining families from the Durham coalfields, the closure of the Somerset & Dorset Railway in 1966 signalled the end of mining in the region, as transportation of the coal became difficult and expensive. With the colliery suffering losses a decision was taken to close the pit in 1968. The shafts were in filled using the waste material from the spoil tips, known locally as 'batches'. The last remaining Somerset mine at Haydon, a short distance north of Kilmersdon, closed in 1973 and Somerset lost its coal production for ever. It has been said that vast amounts of black gold still remain buried deep below the Mendip Hills, but the seems are thin and twisted, making them very difficult and expensive to work.

A typical leafy lane of the Nettlebridge Valley.

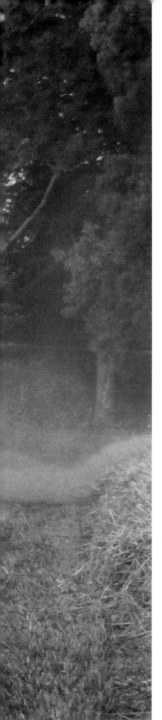

A classic harvesting scene close to Stratton-on-the-Fosse.

The winding lanes bordered by ancient hedgerows and the broad-leafed wooded valleys of eastern Mendip are delightful at any time of year, continuously changing with the seasons. Winter sees them in their dormant stage, ready to withstand the inevitable westerly gales, while in spring they become alive with the promise of new growth. Summer draws them into full bloom, but it is early autumn when they inevitably look their best. Most of the species of trees found in the British Isles are linked to folklore that can be traced back centuries. One such exception is the sycamore, which was introduced into Britain in the 1500s. Today, the sycamore is one of the most common trees to be seen across the landscape. During autumn sycamore seeds are ready to be dispersed on the gentlest of breezes, designed to travel some distance from the tree. Each half is made up of the fruit and a flat wing. It is these wings that allow the fruit to travel away from the tree in the wind. Horse chestnut provides one of the first signs that summer is slowly losing ground to autumn, bringing forth the time-honoured conker. It has been suggested that the customary game of conkers was originally called conquerors and was played with the shells of snails.

Hazelnut, sycamore and horse chestnut are all prevalent in eastern Mendip.

Winter transforms the Nettlebridge Valley. The snow and ice produces a winter wonderland, but severe snow and ice can render the country lanes that serve the rural villages on Mendip treacherous to traffic.

The weathervane that adorns the pavilion at Downside deserves a second look.

The Fosse Way, a Roman road running from Exeter to Lincoln, was built during the first century, taking its name from the Latin *fossa*, meaning ditch. The route of the Fosse Way was once the most western point of the Roman occupation of Britain and would certainly have been protected by a defensive ditch. Stratton-on-the-Fosse straddles the Fosse Way, being dominated by the relatively new Benedictine monastery, Downside Abbey, built between 1882 and 1925, with its 166ft-high square tower. The village is also home to the Norman parish church of St Vigor. Stratton-on-the-Fosse was the site of a tragic plane crash which took place in May 1943 on the playing fields at Downside School, when a single-seater plane went out of control, forcing the pilot to bail out. The plane crashed on to the cricket pitch, killing nine schoolboys and injuring several more. The pilot also lost his life that day. Today the cricket pavilion looks resplendent with its red roof and delightful weathervane.

The sound of leather on willow. Stratton 1st XI batting against Bath 3rd XI viewed from pitch level, creating the quintessential English village summer sporting scene. The gentleman seated is taking advantage of the glorious location and a balmy summer afternoon with the temperature regulated by occasional cloudy skies.

I thought I would leave it up to you to decide what happens next. You may just spot the ball perhaps on its way to the stumps.

Downside Abbey provides the most striking of backdrops to the cricket pitch, where during the summer months the sound of leather on willow can be heard. The rules of cricket have always been a source of confusion for the uninitiated, but the following description, its source unknown, tries to explain in detail:

'You have two sides, one out in the field and one in. Each man that's in the side that's in the field goes out and when he's out comes in and the next man goes in until he's out. When a man goes out to go in, the men who are out try to get him out and when he is out he goes in and the next man in goes out and goes in. When they are all out, the side that's out comes in and the side that's been in goes out and tries to get those coming in out. Sometimes, there are men still in and not out. There are men called umpires who stay out all the time and they decide when the men who are in are out. Depending on the weather and the light, the umpires can also send everybody in, no matter if they're in or out. When both sides have been in and all the men are out, including those who are not out, then the game is finished'.

The bleak midwinter has its compensations on mornings such a this, with the low winter sun casting shadows across the frosted countryside while bathing the abbey at Stratton-on-the-Fosse in a warm golden glow.

The roof long gone and clad in ivy, the old barn and agricultural equipment makes for a classic winter scene after a dusting of snow.

All that remains of the original village of Holcombe is the old church of St Andrew, set in the upper reaches of a deep wooded valley.

Holcombe

Holcombe is to be found in the north-east of Mendip, with the highest part of the village just over 640ft above sea level. The original settlement was over half a mile north, although all that remains of the original village is the old church of St Andrew set in the upper reaches of a deep wooded valley. The new village was born from the need to relocate as a consequence of the Black Death when the majority of the villagers succumbed to the plague, with the few survivors moving to the present site.

The Black Death had taken a hold in the Melcombe Regis area of Weymouth in 1348, sweeping through southern England like a raging forest fire. Holcombe has its own legend and it is clear to see why tradition has it that the Holcombe Inn, once called the Ring O' Roses, was said to have taken its name from the nursery rhyme recalling the chilling tale of the plague; the first sign of the plague was said to be a ring of rose-coloured spots. A posy of herbs allegedly offered some protection, but once sneezing had taken hold that would have signalled death was not far away.

Ring a ring o'roses, a pocketful of posies,
atishoo, atishoo, we all fall down.

The legend of Holcombe was told by Father Ethelbert Horne, one-time Abbott of Downside, who in 1905 led the excavations at Nettlebridge, discovering Bronze Age pottery in a cave. The legend tells how the Bishop had ordered all the villagers to their respective churches to pray for deliverance from the plague. All the villagers from Holcombe were congregated at church, all that is except the sexton, who was described as a hunchback and a most unpleasant fellow. He had met a peddler coming down to the village who was in some difficulty, frequently stopping to rest and laying the large pack he was carrying on the ground. It was clear to the sexton he was very weary. On reaching the sexton's hut the peddler sat down and asked for a drink. The Black Death took two forms: one that would result in death within the hour of the first symptom of haemorrhaging, the second in which great black swellings under the arms and groin would appear before death followed a couple of days later. Very few survived and those who did took many months to recover. The sexton gave the peddler a drink but almost at once he started to haemorrhage. Clearly he had the plague.

The sexton is said to have guided him to a shed with a stick, so as not to touch him, and to have taken the large pack to a pond to wash off the blood stains. The peddler died and that night the sexton dragged his body to the pond, weighing him down with large stones to ensure he sank. The next day he claimed that he had collected the large pack from Bristol while they were in the church and started selling the contents for princely sums as a crowd of villagers gathered around. Very shortly the first signs of plague started to take hold

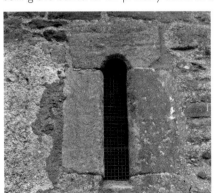

among the population, with death following swiftly. The villagers held prompt services for the victims before a hasty burial in a communal grave, at the southern end of the church. Today all that remains of the original village is the burial mound and the old church of St Andrew.

This tiny window in the church tower is thought to date from Saxon times.

An unusual view looking up at the tower and the Norman arch, a relic of a previous building, providing an attractive entrance to the church.

The pulpit and lectern.

The old church, which has been restored, holds occasional services. Perhaps the most notable name in the churchyard is that of Captain Robert Falcon Scott, 'Scott of the Antarctic'. Although he is not buried there, his name is inscribed on the tombstone of the family grave in the churchyard.

Built in the late Middle Ages, replacing an original Saxon church, the records show that some further works were carried out in the 17th and 18th centuries. The Churches Conservation Trust, the national charity that cares for and preserves churches of historic and architectural interest, looks after 340 churches scattered throughout England, including St Andrew's. It is a simple and unassuming structure on the outside, while inside the wooden Georgian box pews, pulpit and lectern, along with the west gallery, remain much as they would have been almost 200 years ago.

The Georgian box pews with the west gallery beyond remain much as they were when built.

A glorious sunrise over eastern Mendip. With the hills decreasing in height from west to east the landscape allows for some awe-inspiring scenes at dawn.

Early morning autumnal mist engulfs the small hamlet of Charlton on the north-eastern slopes of Mendip.

Kilmersdon

Autumn is frequently described as the 'season of mellow fruitfulness', when early morning mists collect in the valleys, river beds and frost hollows, creating a seemingly timeless and mysterious landscape. Here mist engulfs the small hamlet of Charlton on the north-eastern slopes of Mendip and the lower lying valleys below the hills. Mist occurs when the moisture in the air turns to fine vapour droplets caused by the temperature falling to what is known as the dew point. A less romantic description of the early morning autumnal mists is 'radiation fog'. Close to Charlton is the village of Kilmersdon, nestled in a deep valley bordered on all sides by rich farmland and broad-leafed woodlands. Unlike its near neighbouring villages of Holcombe and Mells, Kilmersdon shows very little sign of any significant early mining or industrial activity, with a definite lack of gruffy ground. The picturesque village, however, is a wealth of architectural delight. The road descends steeply from Charlton and on entering the village the first house you see at the foot of the hill was originally the tollhouse, part of the turnpike network of Somerset.

Ploughing creates a classic autumn scene close to Charlton, with the seagulls having a field day in more ways than one.

The early morning mist will soon melt away as the winter sun begins to strengthen.

During the mid-1700s, with increased traffic on the tracks or roads, an Act of Parliament was passed that allowed local people to set up Turnpike Trusts to raise money to build, repair and maintain these increasingly vital arteries between settlements. To enable the trusts to recover these costs they were at liberty to charge a toll for their use depending on the size of carriages and the number of horses. All foot travellers and Royal Mail coaches were exempt from these charges. The tolls were collected at turnpikes or tollhouses. Agriculture has always been the village's main source of industrial activity apart from a brief period in history. From the late 19th century agriculture was overtaken by mining as a rich seam of coal was discovered under Kilmersdon. At the height of the coal-mining era in the late 1950s a substantial pit had been developed. A shaft 875ft deep had been sunk at nearby Haydon in 1874, with several miles of tunnels leading underground below Kilmersdon. With nationalisation of the coal industry the mine became a significant source of coal production, but as with all of the Somerset coalfield costs increased and demand eventually declined, with closure coming in 1973. This put an end to coal mining in Somerset.

Mileposts were compulsory on all turnpikes to inform travellers of direction and distance and to help coaches keep to their schedule. This one at Kilmersdon guided travellers on the road from Wells to London.

105

The tollhouse at Kilmersdon was built in around 1825. When the road was straightened the toll house was moved from the top of the hill to its present position.

Kilmersdon shares with its close neighbours Holcombe and Mells an association with a nursery rhyme. Kilmersdon is the home of Jack and Jill. The rhyme goes:

Jack and Jill went up the hill,
To fetch a pail of water,
Jack fell down and broke his crown,
And Jill came tumbling after.

Up got Jack, and home did trot,
As fast as he could caper,
He went to bed and bound his head,
With vinegar and brown paper.

Jack and Jill's hill begins its ascent close to the parish church and is clearly signed, with a well at the top of the hill in the grounds of the village school. Slate plaques on the school walls reveal the full explanation of the events of the time. The exact location of the original hill described in the rhyme is believed to be close by in a copse a little way from the school. The well has been subject to archaeological surveys, which revealed that it is of medieval origin, and the hill above the village was once home to 'bad stone quarry', now filled in after it was shut down due to rocks rolling down the hillside into the village.

To the hill. The sign points the way to the top of the hill, but take care not to fall.

The purpose of nursery rhymes is often debated. It is suggested that they were simple moral medieval tales with words that could be set to music and easily remembered by the whole village. Many theories abound as to the origin of this story, but a local saying goes that in these parts a popular surname is Gilson, derived from 'the son of Jill'. A census was carried out and revealed that 32 families within five miles of the parish church had the surname Gilson.

The plaque on the wall of the school tells the story:

'It is said that centuries ago Jack and Jill daily went up the hill to fetch water. One fateful day Jack was hit by a boulder from nearby bad stone quarry. He tumbled down and suffered a wound that not even vinegar and brown paper could mend. Jill also died young, but not before she had given birth to the couple's son, whom villagers raised and called Jill's son. The surname Gilson still features widely in this area.

An annual Wassail takes place in the village of Kilmersdon on the closest Saturday to the old Twelfth Night, 17 January. The ceremony is thought to date back to at least Anglo-Saxon times, with connections to a pagan ritual. Wassail is derived from Anglo-Saxon 'wass hael' meaning 'be in good health', hence the saying 'hale and hearty'.

Professional wassailers would have travelled from farm to farm, to be paid in food and cider. The ceremony, which was revived in Kilmersdon in 2003, begins with music and Morris dancing followed by the crowning of the new Wassail Queen.

The queen heads a parade through the village to the apple orchard, where a piece of toast is placed in the branches of an apple tree for Robin Goodfellow, the good spirit of the orchard. The wassailing continues with the queen pouring cider all around the roots of the tree as an offering to the spirits, asking for a good harvest.

A cup of mulled cider and brandy is passed around the encircled crowd, with another lively performance from the Morris Men. Many versions of the traditional Wassail song can be heard throughout Somerset and Dorset. The Kilmersdon Wassail song begins with this first verse and chorus as follows:

Dappled shade on the school at the top of the hill overlooking Kilmersdon, where a slate plaque reveals the full story of Jack and Jill. Close by is the site of the original well.

The queen with the traditional communal Wassail cup.

To thee, to thee old apple tree,
Be growth so strong and true,
So fair of blossom and sweet of fruit,
Be yours the season through.

We'll Wassail thee, old apple tree,
And bless thee through the year,
And raise a glass of the goodly brew,
'Good luck' to all of us here.

The Wassail incantation is said with full gusto, ending with a resounding 'Hoorah! Hoorah! Hoorah!' A shotgun is fired to ensure the ritual has not gone unnoticed. Noise is an important element in warding off the evil spirits who could spoil the harvest, while it can also awaken the good spirits from the deep midwinter.

Here's to thee old apple tree, long may thee bud long may thee blow, may thee grow apples enough, hats full, caps full bushel bushel bags full and my pockets full too, Hoorah! Hoorah! Hoorah!'

The shotgun is discharged to ward off evil spirits and to awaken the good spirits.

The Wassail Queen pours the cider.

Shotguns and a flagon of cider are central to the ceremony.

The Morris style of dancing is vigorous and includes enthusiastic 'sticking' – a habit which results in an abundance of firewood! A close look at the one in the middle suggests another is going that way.

Bells are an essential part of the Morris Men's kit.

Morris dancing probably dates back to customs that were around in pre-Christian times, linked to ancient fertility rites, although the origins are disputed. Records dating back to the 15th century suggest that 'Morris' is derived from the French 'morisgue' meaning dance. Other theories suggest that they are linked to the clowning of court jesters, with the tradition passed on for pleasure. The characters associated with the dance, the Fool, the Hobby Horse, the Green Man and the Man-Woman, often referred to as Betty, may give credence to this claim.

Cam Valley Morris Men were formed in 1981 by dancers who had already gained experience with other Morris groups. Today they dance the Morris not only to pass on the tradition, but also for enjoyment, which has probably been the case throughout history. The green of their crossed baldricks and rosettes represents the Valley and the blue the waters of the Cam in Somerset.

Dominating the rural landscape is Ammerdown Estate, home to the Jolliffe family, who became title holders of the village in 1780. The Park, as it became known, was enlarged in 1843, necessitating the diversion of several roads, as had been the case when it was first built in 1791. The Ammerdown Estate today is run by the second son of Lord and Lady Hylton, who still retain the surname Jolliffe. The connection with the Jolliffe family is still prominent in the village, as the inn retains the name the Jolliffe Arms.

Kilmersdon nestles in a deep valley bordered on all sides by rich farmland and broad-leafed woodlands.

Kilmersdon Walk

Distance: 11 miles with an estimated time of 5–6 hours.

Most of this walk follows quiet country lanes, with a section through a wooded valley at Holcombe and the return leg from Vobster to Kilmersdon over undulating Mendip countryside. The walk provides for a full day's excursion, beginning with a long steady ascent before reaching Holcombe, with pubs found in Holcombe, Vobster and Kilmersdon. Parking is easy at the village hall car park in Kilmersdon, where the walk begins at grid reference 696 522.

Turn right for a short distance then right again into Hoares Lane, where you continue with a steady climb for one mile until reaching Luckington Cross, where you bear right, signposted Holcombe. Continue on the unclassified lane for a further mile until you reach a staggered junction. Take the road almost straight on, again signposted Holcombe. You are now in Brewery Lane, which takes its name from the brewery that once dominated the centre of the village until its closure in 1900. This short section along Brewery Lane needs care, so ensure you face oncoming traffic. After just under half a mile, on the outskirts of Holcombe, take the right-hand turn into Dark Lane and at the next junction, with Charlton Road, turn left. In a short distance take the next right fork, where a signpost to Holcombe Old Church Only points the way.

A brewery was established at Holcombe in 1800. A small flooded quarry with a spring that comes to the surface was used as the water supply for brewing, giving the beer a delicacy of flavour. Now a haven for wildlife, the shaft is still visible that once connected to the old pump house to supply the brewery. The last manager of the brewery was John Scott, father of Captain Robert Falcon Scott and grandfather of Peter Scott, who founded the Wildfowl Trust at Slimbridge. There is a tale of a tragic accident at the brewery when a worker was overcome by fumes, falling into a vat of beer and drowning. The story continues to say the brew was not wasted.

Holcombe St Andrew. The old church was built in the late Middle Ages, replacing an earlier Saxon church.

The road to the site of the original settlement at Holcombe.

The walk continues, descending a quite track to the tiny church of St Andrew where the original village of Holcombe once stood. A path runs outside the left wall of the churchyard to begin its descent to the wooded valley. On entering the wood take the left path, which will bring you to the valley floor, crossing the river over an old stone bridge before climbing upwards to a emerge from the wood. Cross the field to the gap straight ahead where a sometimes muddy track will bring you once again onto a lane. Turn left following the lane, but as before on Brewery Lane extra care is needed on this section. After just over half a mile you reach the Holcombe Inn, perhaps for a well-deserved rest, before continuing to the village crossroads. Turn right at the crossroads and descend Holcombe Hill, turning left at the village shop into Common Lane.

The quiet lane descends to a valley where in just over half a mile, at a junction, a right turn takes a pleasant winding lane. The lane crosses a river at Ham, once the site of a canal that never was. Work had begun during the late 1700s to build a branch of the Somerset & Dorset Canal from Edford, passing under the packhorse bridge here at Ham to connect with Frome to serve the collieries at Stratton-on-the-Fosse and Holcombe. Eight miles were completed before funding ran out in 1803. The coming of the railways in 1874 signalled the end for the canal and the plan was finally abandoned. The lane begins to climb out of the valley, turning left at the T-junction then continuing for almost two miles until a minor crossroads at Soho, where you bear left to begin the descent to Vobster.

The old packhorse bridge at Ham.

The small quarry that once supplied water to the brewery is now a haven for wildlife.

The inn at Vobster.

On reaching Vobster the river is again crossed by a delightful four-arched bridge, built in 1764 close to the next well-deserved rest stop, the Vobster Inn. On leaving the pub turn right at the junction onto the main road, where in a short while a footpath on your left should be taken, bearing right up through the trees to emerge at Upper Vobster Farm. Turn left for a short distance onto the lane then take a well-signposted footpath on your right across relatively flat countryside towards Babington. Cross a quiet country lane, where two pillars point the way northwards following a tree-lined path to reach Babington House, a mile from your destination. The path continues on a track, curving gently westward all the time, keeping Babington House on your left.

The descent back to Kilmersdon now enters a woodland where a fork in the path will lead you to the B3135. Turn left through the gate to follow the road back to the car park. You could take a trip up the hill of Jack and Jill before a well deserved rest at the Jolliffe Arms.

The stone pillars lead the way to Babington.

A track continues toward Kilmersdon, keeping Babington House and church on your left.

Cranmore Station. The immaculate station building, signal box and memorabilia recreate the golden days of steam. They offer an enjoyable experience to generations that never knew the uncomplicated and leisurely experience of travelling by steam train.

East Somerset Railway

We have already seen evidence of the Somerset & Dorset Railway that once crossed the Mendip Hills, linking Bath to Evercreech, and beyond to Bournemouth. Eastern Mendip was also served by a second line, this one skirting the southern flank of the hills. At Cranmore we are still over 600ft above sea level, despite being some 15 miles as the crow flies south-east from the summit at Beacon Batch. Cranmore Station was opened in 1858 as an extension on the Westbury to Weymouth line to connect with Shepton Mallet, with the track extended to Wells in 1862. The route never attracted a vast amount of passenger traffic, eventually becoming part of the Great Western Railway in 1874. The line continued as part of the nationalised British Railways, running until 1963 when sadly passenger services were discontinued, as was the case with many branch lines at that time.

The station platform boasts many original feature from the bygone days of steam, including these milk churns, once a familiar sight in every Mendip village.

Opposite: Great Western Railway 0–6–0 Saddle Tank 813, originally built for the Port Talbot Railway and Docks in 1901. It is seen here running into Cranmore Station after some light shunting duties, and is about to take the first passenger service of the day.

The station remained desolate until 1971, when the artist David Shepherd purchased the site while looking for a home for two steam engines he had bought from British Rail in 1967. He reopened the railway as the East Somerset Railway in 1973 with a short distance of track, now extended toward Shepton Mallet with a new station at Mendip Vale, a distance of two miles.

Far right: Engine 30075 getting up a head of steam. The locomotive was restored at Swanage railway before entering service on the ESR in 2004.

More nostalgic highlights from Cranmore Station.

Cranmore Walk

Distance: 7.5 miles with an estimated time of 3.5–4 hours

A pleasant walk through quiet country lanes and undulating countryside providing a nostalgic look at steam trains and a 19th-century folly. Park in Cranmore at grid reference 668 432, where you could combine the walk with a visit to the East Somerset preserved steam railway.

From the minor junction opposite the East Somerset Railway take the lane south to cross the railway line and in a short distance bear right, signposted Chesterblade. The lane gains height and at the next road junction take another right turn, continuing along this quiet country lane for half a mile before another right turn is required. Continue on for a further mile of delightful country lane walking before turning right, signposted Doulting. Another right turn brings you onto Farm Lane, crossing the railway once again, the bridge providing the perfect spot to watch a passing steam train if you are lucky with the timings.

On reaching Doulting take care to cross the busy A361, turning right for a short distance, than take the first left into Chelynch Road. After half a mile the lane bears sharply right, but here you can take a well-earned rest at the Poachers Pocket before continuing along the lane for a further three quarters of a mile to take a right turn, where the lane descends to the hamlet of Waterlip.

Late afternoon light enhances the idyllic village scene at Cranmore.

The lane south of Doulting provides a perfect view of the bygone age of steam.

Cranmore Tower, a folly built in the 19th century, stands in woodland high above the village of East Cranmore.

At Waterlip cross the road to head steadily up hill for 500 yards to pick up a path on your right. The route then becomes relatively level for a while before a junction with another path necessitates first a right turn and then, in a short distance, a left turn to begin a steady climb towards a woodland.

Take the next left to climb steadily through the deciduous woodland to discover Cranmore Tower, built in the 1860s by Thomas Henry Wyatt for John Moore Padget of Cranmore Hall. The tower stands 148ft tall to provide a panorama of the surrounding countryside, sat as it is on the highest vantage point above Cranmore, 925ft above sea level. It may be just a coincidence, but the height at the top of the tower above sea level is almost at the same altitude as the Mendip summit at Beacon Batch. During the 1930s the attached cottage was used as a tearoom, before the Home Guard during World War Two used it as a lookout. It then fell into disrepair. The tower and cottages have been fully restored and are now in private ownership.

The return to Cranmore begins by retracing your footsteps out of the wood then heading down toward the A361, taking care crossing this busy road. Continue following another path downward though the field to emerge at the entrance to All Hallows School. Turn right onto East Cranmore Lane to follow the lane for just under a mile back to Cranmore with its delightful duck pond, the perfect spot for a well-deserved rest at the Strode Arms or perhaps the Railway Station.

There is debate as to whether they are native to Britain, but snowdrops traditionally herald the end of midwinter and are a sure sign that spring is approaching.

The parish church is Grade I listed and dates from the 12th century.

Nunney

Nunney nestles in a hollow at the most extreme edge of south-eastern Mendip, a little west-south-west of Frome. In modern times the village has been described as 'the prettiest village in England', and with a 14th-century castle, a church dating from the 12th century and a tranquil river running through it is easy to see why. All Saints' Church in Nunney was almost certainly built on the site of a Saxon or Norman church, as is the case with several of the churches visited on our journey through Mendip. The present tower dates from the 15th century. Extensive restoration was carried out in the 19th century.

The castle was designed by John de la Mare under royal licence from Edward III in 1373. It was built in the French style by Sir John, who had returned from the Hundred Years War in France suggesting that it was based on the Bastille in Paris. The castle had a drum tower at each corner, almost touching on the end elevations, with a roof not unlike that of a traditional French chateau. Four floors were located in the tower house, each with a central room, and leading from this were four circular rooms within the towers. Although surrounded by a deep moat, thought to be one of the deepest in England, it lacked a traditional portcullis. The first real attack on the castle resulted in a huge hole being blasted in the north wall by Cromwell's men in 1645, which showed that the walls were unable to withstand cannon fire.

Early morning sun highlighting the castle's mellow Oolite and Bath Stone.

The castle had a drum tower at each corner with a roof resembling a traditional French chateau.

From that day forward the castle was never inhabited again. The castle is mentioned in *Kelly's Directory* of 1902 as 'being overgrown with ivy but with walls of great strength, the side walls being 7 feet 6 inches in thickness and those of the tower 7 feet, and within these are passages and staircases, a moat 22 feet wide and 10 feet deep'. On Christmas day 1910 the north wall finally collapsed, bringing with it most of the remaining interior, which tumbled into the moat. The site is now managed by English Heritage. In 1934 the Great Western Railway commemorated the castle by naming locomotive 5029, one of its Castle Class Locomotives, *Nunney Castle*. The locomotive is now fully restored and a regular visitor to many of the preserved railways throughout the country.

The village of Mells nestles on the eastern slopes of Mendip above the Wadbury Valley.

Mells

The historic village of Mells nestles on the extreme north-eastern edge at the foot of the Mendips. Described as the quintessential English village, several quiet country lanes meet at Mells from the hamlets of Great Elm, Vobster, Egford and the village of Buckland Dinham. Mells has long associations with English literature and architecture, including John Soane, Thomas Hardy, Edward Burne-Jones and Evelyn Waugh. The war poet Siegfried Sassoon is buried in the grounds of the 15th-century parish church. He was awarded the Military Cross for bravery in 1916, which he was to later renounce. He became an outspoken opponent of the war after being admitted to a war hospital suffering from shell shock. It was during his stay in hospital that he was first encouraged to write poetry, which developed in his last years under the influence of Mells and Downside. Sir Edwin Lutyens was a leading 20th-century architect, whose works included The Cenotaph in Whitehall and the rebuilding of Mells Park House in 1925 after the original Soane-designed house burnt down in 1917. He improved the Manor House, the main war memorial and several other structures within the village. There are memorials by Alfred Munnings and Eric Gill to Edward Horner and Raymond Asquith, who died fighting in France.

The Mells River rises high up in the Mendips close to Emborough Pond, meandering through the Nettlebridge valley then continuing on its even passage until reaching Mells itself. A short distance downstream the river took on a significant role during the early Industrial Revolution, transforming the Wadbury Valley with its waters being tapped to power one of the largest producers of edged iron tools in Britain for more than a century. The main route through Mells from Vobster to Great Elm passes Mells Manor, the 15th-century church and the old coaching inn built as a resting place for early travellers on the road from Wells to London.

Low early morning autumn sun strikes Mells Manor and the church while the grounds remain in dappled shade. The entrance to Mells Manor is guarded by two stone pillars crowned with sculptures, said to be of Talbot's, now extinct hunting dogs from the 15th century. The dogs feature on the Horner coat of arms.

Mells has all the classic elements of an archetypal English village, as can be seen in this view from close to the 15th-century Talbot Inn. The inn was originally a coaching inn on the Wells to London road.

Mells contains a wealth of historical and important architectural buildings, remaining much as they would have been centuries ago. It is here that we come across the connection to Holcombe and Kilmersdon, as tradition has it that Mells was the home of Little Jack Horner, he of nursery rhyme fame. The legend goes that Jack helped himself to the deeds of Mells Manor after the Abbott of Glastonbury hid them in an enormous

In 1908 Lady Francis Horner presented the village with two taps. One was here at Woodlands End, being housed in a stone shelter designed by Sir Edwin Lutyens.

The village bus stop must be one of the most picturesque in England, seen here sporting its autumn coat.

Christmas pie baked for King Henry VIII containing the deeds to 12 manors. Jack Horner was given the pie to take to London and while at Mells was said to open the pie and took the deeds to the manor of Mells, the plum in the pie. The rhyme goes as follows:

Little Jack Horner sat in a corner,
Eating a Christmas pie,
He put in his thumb,
And pulled out a Plum
And said 'what a good boy am I'.

The village stores and post office are always regarded as the centre of any thriving rural community, as important as the school and the village pub. Sadly, they are disappearing fast from the villages of Mendip and indeed throughout Britain, but not here in Mells as that trend has been halted. The refurbished stores and post office came from the determination of the villagers, who launched a campaign to keep the village shop open and run it as a community co-op. An appeal to raise funds produced grants from several sources including Somerset Aggregates Levy Sustainability Fund, Mells Parish Council and Whatley Quarry.

Getting the mail to London was once the responsibility of the mail coach, drawn by four horses. First introduced in 1635, passengers could also use the service, but it was designed for speed not comfort, only stopping to pick up the mail. In contrast, the stage coach used the numerous coaching inns for the comfort of passengers and horses alike. The postal service from Somerset to London was said to take about 38 hours.

The *Domesday Book*, commissioned by William the Conqueror in 1085 and completed in 1086, recorded 13,418 settlements across England including Mells, and it records Mells as belonging to the Benedictine abbey of Glastonbury, although not the parish church. It remained so until the Dissolution of the Monasteries and subsequent claiming of the land by Henry VIII in 1539. It was shortly after the dissolution in 1540 that Thomas Horner bought Mells Manor for a large sum, but only later did his descendants move in, where they still remain. The fact that they bought the manor is demonstrable from the original conveyance preserved in the archives. The Jack Horner connection really is a fantasy as Mells was never associated with the rhyme until the end of the 19th century, when a slightly malicious armchair antiquarian in London, who had taken against Frances Horner, dreamt up the connection, as 'Jack' was the name of her husband. The rhyme had first surfaced in the 1370s, some 170 years before the Horners bought Mells Manor. It never appeared again in print until the 1760s, when Jack Horner was firmly located in Barnet, north of London.

Strange as it may seem, it was widespread practice to hide gold, silver and documents on a journey to avoid the highwaymen of the time. Valuables would be concealed being sewn into undergarments or placed inside cakes and pies. The records, however, seem to bear out the fact that the manor was bought and not stolen, but nonetheless the legend remains and creates additional mystery and charm to this historical Mendip village.

The latter-day method of getting the mail to London.

The refurbished village stores and Post Office at the centre of village life.

Close to the upper reaches of the Wadbury Valley the river is swollen by this cascading outfall from Whatley Quarry.

Wadbury Valley Walk

Distance: 2.7 miles with an estimated time of 1.5–2 hours.

Good walking on footpaths through a wooded combe with a rich industrial heritage. Start at grid reference 733 490, east of Mells. An alternative start is at Great Elm, grid reference 791 491. Return to the start point by retracing your steps.

The Wadbury Valley between Mells and Great Elm is a tranquil place rich in flora and fauna with an abundant variety of woodland plants along its sheltered river banks. It is hard to imagine that up to 250 men would have worked here under extreme conditions of noise, smoke and fumes just over 100 years ago.

In 1744 James Fussell III founded the first ironworks at Mells, a tradition that was to continue with following generations until 1894. During the late 1700s the works expanded with the development of a further two mills along the Wadbury Valley between Mells and Great Elm. Development of the ironworking empire continued, adding two more mills near Chantry and one at Nunney. The business was built around the production of high-quality agricultural implements, edge tools, bill hooks, scythes, shovels, spades and axe heads. Fussell had discovered that adding manganese to iron produced steel of a very high quality for edge tools.

The Mells River was the source of power for the tilt hammers and grinding machinery. Up to 11 water wheels were said to have been in use in its heyday, and with the nearby Somerset coalfields supplying the furnaces, all that was necessary for a successful business was close at hand. The ironworks prospered in the early 1800s with the ever-expanding markets of Europe and America being tapped, but by the late 1800s the agricultural market had begun to fall into decline. With demand for tools falling and still reliant on water power the company fell into bankruptcy, eventually being taken over in 1894 by Isaac Nash, with the consequence of the iron production being moved to Worcestershire.

This linear woodland route follows the Mells River as it flows beneath the steep wooded slopes of the Wadbury Valley. The valley's rich heritage, dating back to the early Industrial Revolution, is still very much in evidence, with much of the original infrastructure still clearly visible during this delightful gentle walk. In stark contrast to those times the valley today is a peaceful haven with abundant ferns, mosses and a carpet of wild garlic in early spring. The linear walk through the woodland is best begun a short distance due east of Mells, although parking is very limited. An alternative starting point is close to the mill pond at Great Elm, this time heading up the valley. On entering the woodland just outside of Mells there is no clue to the evidence of past industrial activity that greets you further down the valley.

Hart's tongue fern can be seen in abundance throughout the valley. Described as a plant that grows wild in shady areas, often forming large clumps at the base of trees, it is also found among rocks and riverbanks.

The Mells River is close at hand to your right as the woodland canopy becomes more dense. Come this way in autumn and the distinct aroma of decaying leaves and damp wood is a pleasure to the senses. The well-marked bridleway takes a gentle curve to the left revealing several massive stone outcrops, the first evidence of industrial activity.

The delightful woodland walk continues to descend into the valley with the sound of rushing water ahead confirming that you are close to a cascading outfall from Whatley Quarry. Groundwater is pumped to the river to replenish underground aquifers. On reaching the cascading outlet, fed from the quarry high above, the river becomes your companion for much of the remainder of the journey through to Great Elm. A short distance from the outlet is Mells Sink, a fissure in the rock that allows the water to sink when river levels are high and acts as a spring when levels are reduced. The woodland trail continues and evidence of man's association with the valley can be seen with a small stone building on the river bank thought to have once been the site of a sluice.

Ferns are abundant on the woodland floor, on decaying tree stumps and fallen branches, but look up to the canopy as they are also found growing freely from the densely mossy branches of some trees close to the riverbank. A short distance before the abandoned site of Fussell's ironworks keep to the path closest to the river as the main path skirts the rear of the abandoned buildings, although it would be hard to miss them. On reaching the first of the derelict main buildings you will be pleasantly surprised at how well preserved and substantial they are. The roofs have gone the vegetation is taking over, but they remain solid. The first buildings you come across were believed to have been the manager's offices. It seems that the main area of industrial activity is concealed a short distance further on.

You should prepare to spend a considerable time here exploring the buildings, stone arches, flues and waterways. Steps lead you down to the lower levels close to the river, but care needs to be taken as most of the infrastructure is damp and mossy and very slippery underfoot.

Although this is a gentle walk in comparison to the higher routes on Mendip, a good pair of walking boots is advisable. Spend a while to ponder what life must have been like for the 250 or so men who worked here in harsh conditions over over a century ago.

Easy walking on firm ground beneath the woodland canopy.

Now stripped of most of its buckets and open to the elements, this small waterwheel remains resilient against the passage of time.

Sun shines through the canopy to highlight the stonework on the ivy-clad buildings. The walls are still solid, although the roof and upper floors have long gone.

As you reach the lower levels close to the riverbank take time to explore the relics of a bygone age. Here you can see the labyrinth of stone-clad tunnels and a tail race that was built to feed the water used to power the waterwheels, the infrastructure having withstood the ravages of time. The waterwheels were used in turn to power the tilt hammers and the grinding machines.

The distinctive, subtle aroma of decay is evident in the valley and, as you would expect, an infinite variety of fungi can be seen taking many forms among the living and decaying wood, while toadstools spring up from beneath the carpet of mosses and leaves on the valley floor. Fungus can take many forms, including mushrooms, toadstools and moulds. The plants have no stamens, proper flowers or chlorophyll, taking their sustenance from organic matter.

On leaving the abandoned buildings and relics of past industrial activity the path leads on towards Great Elm and the Lower Wadbury Valley. The walk is a nature lover's delight, with the river close and accessible for the rest of the journey. As you leave behind the past a greater diversity of plants and woodland species are to be found. The river continues gently on its journey, sometimes tumbling over rocks but never far away. The path continues through the steep wooded valley with occasional glimpses of the past, almost hidden from the resultant growth of ivy and mosses. Close to Great Elm the river takes a sharp turn, in contrast to its meandering through the valley, crossed at this point by a wooden bridge. The path now hugs the river for the remainder of the journey to Great Elm.

On reaching Great Elm the walk subsequently retraces your steps, returning up the valley by the same route to the start point, marvelling at the sights that went unnoticed on the outward journey. An alternative would be to continue walking beside the river as it meanders lazily through the tranquil wooded Lower Wadbury Valley for a while longer, discovering more hidden industrial relics, miniature waterfalls and bridges, before deciding to return.

The tranquil valley around the abandoned ironworks betrays to this day the evidence of past industrial activity, as the essential equipment of the day was left abandoned to Mother Nature. The craftsmanship, however, is clear to see.

Toadstools and fungi spring up from beneath the carpet of mosses and leaves on the valley floor.

Evidence of the significance of the river to the ironworks can still be seen.

The church, tower and sundial at Great Elm.

Great Elm

The small village of Great Elm above the Wadbury Valley between Mells and Frome signifies the end of the journey across the Mendip Hills, arriving at its eastern edge. Great Elm was originally a mediaeval village with the church of St Mary Magdalene dating from the 12th century at its centre. Over many centuries the sundial was used to tell the time, and they became a prominent architectural feature on many churches. One can still be seen today on the church tower here at Great Elm. The origin of the sundial almost certainly dates back to prehistoric times when stone rows or circles were used as astrological calendars. The sundial operates on the basis that the shadow of the gnomon or pointer moves from one side to the other as the sun moves across the sky during the day. The earliest mechanical clocks required sundials alongside to adjust their rather inaccurate time-keeping. As late as the 1800s the sundial was gradually replaced as the recognised timepiece with the mechanical clock becoming more accurate and readily available.

The uninterrupted view across eastern Mendip can bring forth some dramatic sunrises.

We have now reached the eastern extent of the Mendip Hills and the end of our journey, having criss-crossed the limestone plateau from west to east. The vast diversity of the landscape and the quintessential villages with their fascinating history have provided an exhilarating experience seen at differing times of the year, all within a relatively small area of Somerset, but one that has still left many tales untold and many places to visit. Villages and hamlets such as Ashwick, Binegar, Leigh on Mendip and Stoke St Michael are still to be discovered, along with the villages that have grown up at the foot of the hills, where the life-giving waters of Mendip emerge as springs. I trust you have enjoyed the journey and it has inspired a visit to the beautiful Mendip countryside.